AFTER THE STORM

By Wendy Parker

Illustrations by Alexandra Parker

This book is dedicated to my dear friends who helped me reach the children of New Orleans after Hurricane Katrina

Caroline Mains

Karen Arndt

the late Pastor Gary Arndt

Herbie Hedgehog was playing on the grass with his hedgehog friends. Herbie felt as cheery as could be and he enjoyed his fellow playmates, as he was a very friendly hedgehog.

Little did he know what was coming----

The very next day the storm hit with rain, fierce winds, lightning, and thunder. It was a terrible hurricane.

Then the floods came, washing away homes and roads, and soaking everything.

After the storm passed, Herbie popped out of his hiding place. To his surprise, the world was completely changed. Trees were knocked down and water was everywhere. Plants were washed away. Not a friend nor animal was in sight. Herbie couldn't even hear a bird singing.

Frightened at first, Herbie thought to himself, *This is very scary. Where is everybody*?

Soon, Herbie decided that since he was a very friendly fellow, he would set out and look for other animals that were in need of help.

And so he did.

As he walked down a very damp path, Phoebe Frog came hopping by. She was confused and jumped especially high when she saw Herbie.

"Oh! You scared me—but then, everything looks scary today."

"Why are you so jumpy?" asked Herbie.

"I'm so nervous," she replied. "What went on here?"

Herbie explained, "There was a terrible storm. You have reason to be nervous. Are you all right?"

"I guess so," replied Phoebe, "but I've lost my lily pad. It was my home, my special place to sit and watch the trees by day and the stars at night." She hopped nervously while she talked.

"That's too bad," said Herbie. "I lost my home too. Would you like to come with me and see if we can find any others who have been upset by this storm?"

"The company would be nice," said Phoebe. "Let's go."

So off they went. The two spent the night huddled against a tree.

The next day, early in the morning, Herbie and Phoebe heard a voice off the path.

"Where are the bananas? I've got to have a banana!"

"Who's there?" shouted Herbie.

"I thought I was the only one still around." replied Miguel Monkey. "Where did you come from. Did you take away all the bananas?"

Herbie introduced himself and Phoebe.

Phoebe said, "No we didn't take away your bananas. The hurricane and floods did that. We lost our homes in the storm. We are looking for others in trouble too. Maybe we could work together and help each other out." She hopped about some more.

"Can you sit still?" asked Miguel. "You are hopping like a nervous twit. Ha Ha!"

"I can't help it," said Phoebe. "This storm has made me so worried."

"Well," said Miguel, "If there were a tree around, I could hang by my tail and make you both laugh—I'm good at that-- but there are no trees. Gone. Blown down. But worse, there are no bananas, and I'm getting so hungry!"

“You could come with us, and we could all look for food and shelter,” suggested Herbie.

So the three journeyed on together.

The trail was wet and soggy. Mold was growing everywhere and it smelled bad!

"Pee-yew," announced Phoebe. "What a miserable place our world has become."

A mile further on, Miguel heard someone crying. "Do you hear that?" he asked the others.

Then they all heard it—Gordon Gorilla was weeping.

"What's the matter?" asked Miguel.

Gordon looked at the group of animals and cried some more. "Leave me alone. My friends are all gone. They left with the storm. Nobody cares about me!"

"That is so sad," said Herbie, "But come with us, and maybe we can get through this storm together."

Gordon replied, "Leave me alone. You don't want me. I'm so sad. I'll just make all of you feel worse. You go on without me."

"No," said Herbie. "We understand why you are sad—it's okay. We need everyone we can find—please come."

So Gordon decided to join the animals, since they didn't mind his crying now and then.

The group walked on.

A short while later, through some trees, Wilma Wolf spied the creatures.

She growled at them, “Get out of here!”

Herbie went to talk to her. “Has the storm bothered you too? Do you have a place to stay?” he asked kindly.”

Wilma chased the little hedgehog off, growling fiercely.

I guess I need someone a little bigger here, thought Herbie. *Gordon Gorilla could handle this better. I'll get him.*

Gordon's huge size quieted the wolf. “What's the problem here?” asked Gordon.

“You all are just here to cause me trouble,” yelled Wilma. “”I have no den to sleep in. The rain and wind washed it away, and now you are making things worse! GRRR”

Gordan replied calmly, “I think you are just as upset about the storm as the rest of us are. That's why you are so angry. Why don't you join us while we try to help each other out?”

“GRRR,” answered Wilma. “I can't help your group. I get so mad, I just growl and scare everybody. You better move on without me.”

Just then, little Miguel Monkey jumped up on Gordon's shoulders, and started to growl like a wolf—in his tiny voice,

"GRR, I'm going to eat you up!" Copying the wolf, he looked so ridiculous, the whole group started laughing, including Wilma!

"Oh all right," said Wilma, "I guess I'll join you, if you can put up with my grumpiness. Staying here by myself won't help, and Miguel is funny."

GRRRR

After a long hike, the group came to a field, with a small stream running through it. The ground was drying out. There were a few trees still standing, and some small hills. The animals decided to rest a bit.

Phoebe Frog, however couldn't sit still—still nervous, you know. Since she couldn't relax, she decided to hop around and look for some things the group might use.

When she returned, she approached Gordon Gorilla, Gordon, there's a pile of trees and logs over there. I was thinking, maybe you could make them into a new den for Wilma Wolf."

Gordon looked up. "I'm still so sad. Sob, sob. But yes, I can move those trees. It will give me something to do."

So Gordon pushed and pulled at the logs and made a fine new den.

"Let's show it to Wilma," said Phoebe, getting excited.

"Hey Wilma, come and see your new home."

Wilma was growling in her usual grumpy way, but she looked over the den.

"Well, it's not like my old den, I liked my old den. This is different."

She started to walk away. Then she saw Gordon, starting to smile for the first time in a long time.

"The old is gone." she said. "This place is dry and very sturdy—maybe I could make a new home for myself here."

"Thank you Gordon." and she managed to say it without growling.

Phoebe Frog was happy that Wilma had a place to stay.

"How I wish I had a lily pad again," she sighed.

"Well Phoebe," declared Gordon, "I can't get you a lily pad. There aren't any around here. But I could roll that big log over there into this stream. Then you would have a place to sit."

"Could you do that for me?" asked Phoebe.

Gordon moved the log for her, and Phoebe hopped onto it. That night she enjoyed watching the stars from her new place. She remembered to thank Gordon for his help.

The next morning, Herbie asked Phoebe, who wasn't quite so nervous anymore, if she could hop around and see if there was any food for Miguel. The little monkey was tired of eating leaves, and was still calling out for bananas, though he was keeping everyone laughing with his antics.

"Sure" she replied, "but I will need some help carrying what I find."

Hearing the talking, Wilma came out of her den. "Hop on my back, Phoebe," Wilma offered. "We will look for Miguel's food together."

The two explored the area, and to their surprise, they found some strawberries growing near some trees at the edge of the clearing. They brought some back for Miguel.

"Here," suggested Wilma. "Try some of these, Miguel."

Miguel picked one up and sniffed it.

"In case you haven't noticed," said the monkey, "these are not bananas. I only like bananas. These are red. Are bananas red? No, they are yellow. Now, what am I supposed to do with these?"

Disappointed, Wilma replied, "You could try them. Look, the storm destroyed the bananas. There aren't any around. But you might like these, if you weren't so stubborn."

"Oh, okay." said Miguel. "Since you and Phoebe went to the trouble to gather them for me, I'll try one."

Miguel nibbled at a strawberry.

"Hmm," he said. "It doesn't taste like a banana, and I miss my bananas."

He took another bite. "This berry is sweet, and juicy, and uh, kind of good. Yes, I'll have another. Anyone else want to try one? And thanks Wilma and Phoebe."

Afterwards, Wilma helped Herbie Hedgehog dig a really nice hole for a new home. Herbie was thinking about how the group, working together had overcome a lot of their troubles.

Gordon Gorilla said to Herbie, “You know, I don't cry much any more.”

“I'm glad. What has made you feel happier?” asked Herbie.

“Well,” answered Gordon, “when I lost my friends after the hurricane, I thought I would never have any again and I would always be lonely.

“Now I see I have made new friends—you and Wilma, and Phoebe and Miguel. We have come through a very hard time, and we can stay together and be a new family. If trouble comes, we can help each other.

“And Herbie, you are the one who got us together in the first place. We are all so glad you are such a friendly fellow!”

“Right you are Gordon,” replied Herbie. “We must remember to accept our feelings, and our differences, while we each give what we can—Then we can recover from this old storm.”

And they did!

Wendy Parker is a board certified clinical nurse specialist in child psychiatric and mental health nursing She has thirty years experience working with children and families in the mental health field. Special foci have been child trauma, the problems of poverty, and using storytelling as a therapeutic tool.

She is active in the Littleton Congregational Church, United Church of Christ and through the UCC travelled twice on mission trips to aid in Katrina Recovery.

Ms. Parker is currently working as a medication prescriber for mentally ill children. She resides in Littleton, Massachusetts.

Alexandra Parker was born on March 10, 1994. She currently lives in Lynnfield, Massachusetts along with her parents and older brother. She is currently attending Drexel University as a nursing student. Ever since Allie was young, she always had a passion for sketching and painting. She had a private art instructor, who guided her in becoming a better artist. Allie also participated in several art shows to display and sell her watercolor and oil paintings. Today, she continues to develop her art skills, but has more of a focus on nursing. She has volunteered at Winchester Hospital and Massachusetts General Hospital and is currently working at Anna Jaques Hospital in Newburyport, Massachusetts. "I have finally found the thing that thrill's me the most," say's Allie, "because I get to help people and make a difference in their lives!"

AFTER THE STORM

This book began as a puppet show which was devised to address the trauma experienced by preschoolers in the New Orleans area, after Hurricane Katrina of 2004. Following an initial experiment using a puppet to talk to children in January, 2005, I was invited to do a whole show in five different schools during my second trip in April, 2007. The children and teachers responded so favorably to the story, that I wrote it as a narrative when I returned home. This book is intended for use with children who have suffered from a disaster of any kind. My hope is that the story will provide some encouragement for young children who are facing major disruptions in their lives.

In the story, I integrated theoretical background from the fields of trauma work, grief work, and play therapy.

Working with the children and adults in Katrina Recovery has been an amazing and rewarding experience. Combining artistic expression in story telling with expertise in child mental health nursing proved to be a creative way to address trauma and loss.

Special thanks to my husband, Jim Potter, for his help in the production of this book.

Wendy Parker, MS, RNCS

Made in the USA
Charleston, SC
14 November 2012